Guillain-Barre Syndrome

My Journey Back

By Shari Ka

Order this book online at www.trafford.com
or email orders@trafford.com

Most Trafford titles are also available at major online book retailers.

Printed in the United States of America.

ISBN: 978-1-4269-6127-4 (sc)
ISBN: 978-1-4269-6128-1 (e)

Trafford rev. 04/25/2011

 www.trafford.com

North America & international
toll-free: 1 888 232 4444 (USA & Canada)
phone: 250 383 6864 ♦ fax: 812 355 4082

In Loving Memory

Bradley Eugene "Brad" Bushman
Brad was a Deputy Sheriff for the Tippecanoe County Sheriff's Dept.

Son of Mr. and Mrs. Harry Bushman

I dedicate this book to Brad Bushman and all others that have lost their lives to Guillain-Barre Syndrome and to those who are dealing with the complications of Guillain-Barre Syndrome.

The names of all the nurses and techs at OHMS and UofL hospitals have been changed due to the difficulty in locating each worker and obtaining permission to use their names in this publication. I used the true names of all others mentioned in this book.

There are so many people that I want to thank. I want to thank Dr. Joyce Haislip for her swift diagnosis of GBS and relentless care. Dr. Haislip will always be my hero!! She sets the example, as to what every physician should be. Dr. Haislip suggested that I write this book and that has been a great encouragement for me to complete this book.

Thank you Teena, one of my nurses at UofL, for your prayers and encouraging me to write this book. You are everything a health care professional should be. Your wonderful care and kindness will never be forgotten.

I wish to thank all of the doctors and healthcare workers at Owensboro Mercy Healthcare Systems and The University of Louisville Hospital. I will never forget the excellent care that I received by such genuinely kind health care professionals. I will never forget each of you. You have a special place in my heart always.

Thank you Farris, for being there for me through the worst time of my life. Farris's assistance with my care in the hospital was beyond all expectations.

Thank you Joe and Joy Erwin, for house and dog sitting. Thank you for the hospital bed and getting everyone together and setting everything up for my return home. You are Angels for sure!! Thank you for the beautiful flowers and the wonderful food. I loved your visits. Most of all, thank you for prayer time each time you left. God heard you.

Thank you Hollis and Hollis Jr., and all others that helped to get the house ready for my return.

Thank you Marilyn, for being there for me when I needed you the most. Not only did you help provide daily care after I returned home, you spent hours talking with me and made me laugh again!! I love you Meddie.

Thank you Cassie, for driving from Kokomo to check on my catheter care. You were there on a day that was my lowest and the talk that you had with me made all of the difference. Your kind words that day changed a dark mood to food for thought that I have carried with me from that day on.

Thank you Brenda, for setting up my medicine schedule and all that you have done and do. You are a Godsend.

Thank you Kelley, for the physical and message therapy. I know that your caring skills are the reason that I bounced back in record time. Thank you for giving me the confidence to take those first steps!!

Thanks to Farris's family, for all the visits and wonderful food that you regularly brought by. It made all of the difference!! You are all wonderful people and I will never forget all of your loving kindness.

Thank you Crystal, for every caring thing that you did for me. Your compassion and kindness will never be forgotten. You truly are a very special person.

Thank you Jim and Jane Erwin, for clearing the snow from our driveway, so the ambulance could bring me home. You are such wonderful neighbors.

Thank you Jerry and Lorene, Dick and Elaine and Emmett, for your many visits, cards and phone calls. I love you

Thanks to all of my friends and families that visited me while I was in the hospital and after I returned home. Every prayer, card, phone-call and visit meant more to me than I can say. The out-pouring of love was an important part of my recovery.

Each person gave in his or her own special way. I will always have a special place in my heart for each of you. Your kindness will never be forgotten.
You are all in my prayers.

I received a newsletter from the **Guillan-Barre/CIDP Foundation**. Accompanying the newsletter was a list of liaisons, which have experienced GBS or CIDP on a personal level.

One of the contacts in the newsletter is Jonathan. I called Jonathan and left a message of my interest in talking with him. Jonathan returned my call and we talked for quite some time about GBS.

Jonathan shared his experiences with GBS, as well as I shared my experiences with him. He talked with me with genuine interest and I can't explain how comforting and encouraging that one phone call was and is to this day.

With GBS one does not know if there will be a complete recovery from the disease. Every patient recovers differently, as well as the amount of time it may take for recovery, varies with each individual. Some folks die from the disease, some remain paralyzed the remainder of their lives, some only partially recover and some recover completely. Most times the outcome of recovery is determined by the severity in which one has the disease.

Jonathan is the only person that I have talked with that had GBS. He became ill with GBS several years ago as a young man with a young family. Jonathan had a very severe case of GBS. He was in a coma and on a respirator. Jonathon shared with me that he has completely recovered. He related that it took him at least 2 years to recover completely.

Talking with one that knows my daily challenges and concerns of GBS was a Godsend. So many times I have told myself that this is probably the best that I am going to be, because it has been a year since my illness started. I am o-k with that, but I do want to be better and back to the physical abilities I had before GBS. Jonathan shared with me that he is completely recovered with the exception of some numbness in his feet. I was ecstatic to hear that. There is good reason for me to hope that I too, may completely recover. I was hopeful of complete recovery before I talked with Jonathan, yet after one year; I was beginning to be doubtful of my own recovery. Since I talked with Jonathan I have a new anticipation that I too will continue to recover beyond where I am today.

Encouragement

Guillain-Barre Syndrome has been a journey I did not wish to take. It has been a journey that I never imagined would ever happen to me. Many days have been difficult with one struggle after another. If I have learned anything in my years of living, it is that we cannot change what is, we can only deal with what is, the best we can and continue to push forward, although at times it may be, but an inch a day. Never quit!! Fight to be the best you can be in all things. Change, such as being struck down with Guillain-Barre Syndrome or any illness can be life altering, but it doesn't have to defeat you. Fight and allow nothing to defeat you. I mean that from the depths of my soul. When dealing with these kinds of challenges, keep your visions positive and your focus on a healthier tomorrow. You may have to accept change and that change may be hard, but never allow the thought "impossible" entertain your outlook. Defeat is real sometimes, but it can be only temporary if you don't accept it and don't allow it to stay. Physically I am different since Guillain-Barre Syndrome, yet I am still me, but in so many ways better. My body heart and soul has changed… I am better… I am stronger and better.

I did not want Guillain-Barre, yet this illness didn't give me the luxury of choice, as with most illnesses. A year has past and today when I give thought as to what good I can take with me, what good have I learned from this experience? I have learned what others have been dealing with and experiencing for years. I have learned to be a helpless, paralyzed person, although temporary, I now know what this kind of dependence can be to one's every waking minute. I know what a baby feels when they are trying to walk. I know all of the struggles, fears and triumphs of learning to do the simplest things that most of the population does autonomically. I know both worlds, the able bodied and the severely handicapped person's world. Guillain-Barre Syndrome did not become who I am. I learned through it all, I am still me, I am still me, I truly am a better me in all that I am.

My prayer for you, who are struggling with life's challenges, is that you keep looking ahead and know that God and His helping Angels are with you always. There are many things that happen that we won't understand; yet we are never alone. At your darkest hour, He is ever there and He is cradling you.

Love Yourself

God is the Master painter, Sculptor, Poet and you are His signature. He created you with a passionate love beyond understanding. Focus on this truth with your entire being. Embrace your life as the gift that it is. Cherish your qualities with absolute awareness of your uniqueness. You are one and never to be duplicated. Is that not proof enough of your importance to God and His plan for all life, your life?

How few know that we are to love ourselves. By that I do not mean, as the world loves, for that is vanity. Vanity only manifests conceit. Vanity has no real worth, no depth. Vanity is false… merely a pretense. Vanity is a mask to cover truth. Vanity is a corrupt thief that can steal away God's purposes.

The love that I speak of is the love that comes from the knowledge that your life is a gift. Your journey in life is the unwrapping of that gift and maturing to a place to know and appreciate with awe the spirit of you…to learn God's purposes for you. To love yourself is to understand the meaning of life… your life.

I try to focus on the positives of life; therefore I am speaking to you concerning goodness and reasons for being. What joy and peace one can know with the loving acceptance of self. With the realization of one's self-worth one can grow…become and be what God intended.

God is the Master Painter, Sculptor, Poet and you are His signature. He created all things with perfection and you are a part of His perfect masterpiece.

By: Shari Ka, 2001

Guillain-Barre Syndrome or GBS

Guillaine-Barre Syndrome is a disorder that causes damage to the peripheral nerves. The peripheral nerves send messages from the brain to the muscles, instructing the muscles to move. These nerves carry pain sensations from the body to the brain. GBS nerve damage often causes muscle weakness and sometimes this is to the point of paralysis. There can be problems with sensation, including pain, tingling, crawling skin or certain amounts of numbness.

Guillain-Barre is a medical emergency when the weakness affects the chest muscles responsible for breathing. If the chest muscles become paralyzed, the patient can die from the lack of oxygen. Those who have been diagnosed with Guillain-Barre Syndrome must be carefully monitored in a hospital to be sure that all vital functions are maintained.

Guillain-Barre is an autoimmune disorder. The body's immune system attacks and destroys the myelin sheath, which is the covering for the long nerve cell bodies. It is much like the insulation on an electrical cord. The myelin protects the nerve and helps speed the electrical impulses down the nerve. If the myelin is destroyed the nerves impulses travel very slowly and sometimes are disrupted. If muscles do not get the proper stimulation through nerve impulses, the muscles will not function properly.

The cause of GBS is not known, yet it is thought that the immune system is trying to fight an infection such s bacteria or a virus, then accidentally injures nerve tissue in the process.

Why GBS affects some people is a mystery. In more than two-thirds of patients, **GBS occurs one to three weeks after a viral disease, such as a common cold, or flu**. The most common infectious trigger seems to be a bacterial infection with **Campylobacter jenuni**, which causes intestinal infections.

Sometimes GBS follows immunization, surgery or bone marrow transplantation. Research for Guillain-Barre Syndrome is ongoing.

Symptoms vary from person to person. Symptoms can range from mild to severe. The most common and most often first symptoms are weakness in feet and/or feet and legs. With time the weakness can involve the arms, legs and head. It can affect speech and eyes. Sometimes the first symptoms are a tingling, usually in the feet and legs. The tingling can be accompanied by pain. GBS can impair the body's blood pressure.

GBS progresses very quickly, with the worst weakness in the legs, arms, chest, and any other muscle group, within three weeks of the start of the disease. GBS can become complete paralysis with-in hours or a few days. **Any person developing a sudden weakness in the legs and arms should contact a doctor immediately.**

Regaining pre-illness functioning can take months or years. The weakness or paralysis of GBS may last days, weeks, months or years. This varies with each person affected by GBS.

Most people are hospitalized, because the disease can weaken the chest muscle to the extent that breathing is difficult or impossible. If chest muscle is weakened, then a patient is often times put on a respirator. When a patient experiences paralysis of legs and other muscle groups the patient will require supportive care for eliminating waste, psychological support, pain management, blood pressure monitoring and physical therapy.

The two treatments that are used to help speed recovery are **plasmapheresis** and infusions of **immunoglobulin**.

Plasmapheresis: This is a process in which the blood is removed from the body, then separated into plasma and blood cells. The blood cells are put back into the body. The body makes more plasma to replace what has been removed. Scientists believe this treatment works by removing substances that contribute to the immune system's attack on the peripheral nerves.

Immunoglobulin Infusions: This is a mix of antibodies that are produced naturally by the body's immune system. High doses of immumoglobulin may work by blocking the antibodies that may have caused this disease.

Angels Everywhere

Angels are ever there, to guide you through your day and guard you in stillness of night. They speak with silent words, which slip into your thoughts, a moment of awareness you may not identify... it is your Angels and they are ever at your side.

God sent His loving messengers, assigned to you at birth. His Angels are to protect and keep you, all your days on earth. Angels everywhere, always showing that they care... you are not alone, for Angel's work is never done. When you sense a warming presence, 'tis your Angels very near... a sudden thought of danger...'tis Angel's silent speaking... a warning you will hear.

Look about... you will see Angels everywhere. A tiny little baby, with a face so sweet, the softness of a bunny or a hungry, homeless man with nothing to eat. A sudden act of kindness from a stranger's hand, at a moment when you need one to understand. Angels have many faces to show you how they care... yes, they are ever near... many times you have entertained Angels..., so unaware.

By: Shari Ka 2004

We have just finished taking down and boxing up the decorations from the Christmas Holiday Season. Christmas is a time of year that I love. My family is far away and I don't get to see much of them at the Holidays, which means I go through the Holidays feeling a void, yet each year I feel that old familiar Christmas spirit, just as I did as a child.

Although the Holiday Season has past, I have decided to create some recipes for candy. I have been carrying these ideas for recipes around in my head for quite some time. I haven't felt the need to make candy in years! I assemble all of my ingredients on the kitchen counter and away I go!! My favorite creation is graham crackers covered with crunchy peanut butter, top that with a marshmallow, then marchino cherries. After this delightful mix is together, I then dip it in a chocolate shell. It is oh so very good!! I packaged them up and passed them out to friends and family and it was a hit! I'm not the best candy maker, yet I had fun putting together these recipes and having them turn out so delicious.

While making the candy, I spent hours standing on my feet. Standing for long periods of time has never been a problem for me, but my legs are feeling very fatigued. It is very uncomfortable, yet I am not one to pay much attention to aches and pains, because they always go away. I casually think that this will pass too, now that I am finished with the candy project. I can rest those weary legs as I snuggle up with a good book next to the fire.

During the months that it is warm outside, that is where I will be from about noon until after dark nearly everyday. During the warm months I neglect to read anything more than the daily newspaper. I have decided to spend this cold, northern Indiana winter next to the fire place, catching up on reading some of the books that I have had laying around and keep promising myself I will get to them.

I have spent a couple of days making candy during the day and the evenings sitting next to the fire getting a good start with reading about Angels. True accounts of Angelic encounters is a topic I find very interesting and good food for thought. As I am sitting with my book, I notice the slightest tingle at the very tips of my fingers on my right hand. Although it is annoying, it comes and goes, so it must be nothing. I have had 2 cervical fusions and tingling fingers is not at all unusual for me. I tell myself that I have probably worked too hard over the summer. My energy level is over the top and I rarely slow down from the time I get out of bed until I am back in bed at night. I honestly forget that my body does have limitations. I have learned to push and ignore those limitations over the years.

As I am sitting by the fire reading, I notice that my toes are now tingling too... the middle toes on my left foot... I am thinking, "this is odd," yet I am not overly concerned. The phone rings and it is my sister, Marilyn. We usually talk on the phone every day. I complain to her about this odd tingling at the tips of my fingers and now my toes. She says that I probably need to keep my feet up while I am sitting in one position for such long periods of time and I agree. I can sit for hours with a good book and rarely move a muscle. Although the tingling is still there, I dismiss it as my punishment for standing all day making candy and the way I work hard, non-stop all summer too. I make a mental note to slow down next summer. I argue with myself that I am not getting younger and I need to be more careful as to how I over work my body sometimes.

I wonder if I am trying to come down with something. Maybe this year will be my turn to catch something, since so many people around me have had the flu and colds. I have had a slight headache and a mild sore throat. I haven't had the flu for about 20 years, but the bugs that are going around these days can make a person seriously ill and there seems to be a lot of it out there.

The next evening finds me again in front of the warm fire with my book about Angels. As I am trying to concentrate on my read, I notice that my entire left foot feels numb. I again reprimand myself, "you have hurt yourself over the summer and this is not good." Marilyn makes her regular evening call and I tell her that my entire foot is now numb and she insists that I need to put my feet up and move around more.

I agree with her assessment, yet I sense there is something unusual about this, but I am still convinced that I have over worked my back over the summer. As the evening progresses, the numbness is creeping into my right foot too. I am beginning to feel uneasy about these symptoms, because they are unlike anything I have experienced before.

I began to have a hard time concentrating on my book, because the numbness seem to progress over the evening. When I stood up to get myself to bed, I noticed that my feet felt heavy, as if I have added weights to them. I promise myself, I will call Dr. Haislip the next day. While in bed, I lay awake noticing that I am having an increasing amount of pain in the area of my ribs. It is a dull, burning, relentless ache.

Each night at bedtime I eat an apple for a bedtime snack. Apples help with digestion, yet I eat apples, because I love them and this helps me fight the temptation of eating typical junk and snack foods, such as chips. The past 2 nights it has been very difficult to swallow the apples. The pieces seem to stick in my throat or move down very slowly. This must have something to do with the sore throat or maybe I should pay more attention and chew it more. I began to ponder the symptoms and question if they are related. I am beginning to think they must be, because the symptoms are unusual and I am having all of them at the same time.

I called Dr. Haislip's office and the receptionist scheduled me for January the 12th, which was 3 days away. I thought that would be fine, yet I sure will be happy to see her. I was beginning to realize that this is not anything I have had before or at least the symptoms are not familiar to me.

I lived in Kentucky for about 4 years. I found 7 wooded and rolling acres of land that I describe as heaven on earth. I designed and built a beautiful Chalet home deep in the woods on my 7 acres of heaven. I had only lived in Kentucky about 2 months and the construction on my home had just gotten to a good start, when I began experiencing sharp pain in my right chest and under my arm. I made an apt. with doctor Haislip. Dr. Haislip's office is in Owensboro, Kentucky and this was my first visit with her.

Dr. Haislip ordered a mammo and after the mammo was done the doctor saw something that needed a closer look, then an ultra sound was immediately done. The results were not conclusive, yet suspect of breast cancer, which ultimately was the final diagnosis. Dr. Haislip told me she would find the best cancer doctors for me and she did. From that time forward, I

7

have always known that as long as Dr. Haislip is my physician, I will, without a doubt have the most intelligent and the best care available.

By the next morning I am beginning to be very concerned, because the heaviness is now in my legs, as well as my feet. My legs feel so weak… almost tired. The pain in my ribs has increased and as well as the pain that is now in my back. It was very hard to sleep that night due to the pain. It is a burning ache and it is getting much worse.

Joy is our neighbor and lives about ½ of a mile from us. Joy is not only a friend; she has become our house and dog sitter when we travel. She is a Godsend to our pets and us. She loves the dogs and they love her. It is wonderful to be able to leave our fur babies and our home and not worry about them.

I called Joy and asked her to watch the dogs for about 3 days, as I thought I would see the doctor, get some medication and/or tests, then have a day to visit with friends and family in the area. Joy came down and we walked downstairs to the basement where we keep our cat and German Shepherd in the winter. As we climbed back up the stairs, I literally had to hold onto the handrail to pull myself up with my arms, because I had no strength in my legs. They felt so heavy. I said nothing to Joy of my symptoms or doctors apt. I still thought it was going to be something simple, although in the back of my mind, I knew I was in trouble. I fought those negative thoughts and told myself I was being silly, not to worry. We arranged to be gone about 3 days. Joy would start caring for the dogs in the morning.

We decided to drive to Owensboro the day before my apt. and stay in a Motel, because I was having a difficult time with the increasing pain. At bedtime I asked Farris to touch my back, because I had reached for by back and could not feel it. When he touched my back, I was alarmed, because I could not feel his touch.

I knew then, this isn't good. That night I slept very little. The pain and the numbness involved my entire rib cage area and all of my back and buttocks. My legs were so heavy and beginning to have a burning sensation.

The drive to Owensboro, Kentucky from Northern Indiana is about 5 ½ to 6 hours. I think that was the longest hours I have ever spent in a car. I couldn't get comfortable and the pain was increasing. Needless to say the night in the Motel room was with out sleep. I think I had convinced myself that I may have MS. I knew by then that I was developing some level of paralysis. The next day couldn't come fast enough for me, because I would be seeing Dr. Haislip and I knew I was in trouble. My apt. was for 1:00 p.m. I called her office and asked if I could get in to see her sooner that day and the receptionist told me I could come in at 11:00.

As soon as I checked into Dr. Haislip's office, I felt better emotionally. I knew I was in good hands with Dr. Haislip. Little did I know that I handed this wonderful doctor such an unpredictable challenge. A challenge that medical science has very few resources to treat, only hypotheses for cause and no known cure. Little did I know that I was in for the fight of my life and the odds of my winning were stacked against me.

I don't recall the questions Dr. Haislip asked me. I told her of my symptoms. The loss of strength, the paralysis in my back, I am unable to urinate, I am constipated and the new symptoms of difficulty swallowing. My arms are feeling weak and my head feels heavy. She excused herself and returned and asked if I minded going straight to the hospital. She gave me some paper work and I went to the hospital and there I was immediately admitted.

Dr. Haislip asked Dr. Shah, a neurologist to see me that day. I will explain what I remember, as I remember the following events. They may not be in the exact order in which they occurred; yet I will relate the events from my own experiences and memory. It felt as if I was in a fog from the time I was admitted until not long before I returned home.

HISTORY OF PRESENT ILLNESS: A couple of weeks ago she had a headaches, she did not feel well. She had a sore throat. She gargled some and then she began having problems with numbness and tingling in her fingers and her hands. Numbness in her feet now up her leg, up into her buttocks, up her back and across her shoulders. She has not had any fever or chills. Her blood pressure is up today. She is in terrible pain all over. She had some Darvocet left over from a surgery she had and so she is taking half of one every 2 hours. She is constipated more than she has been before. Also she has very little urine output. When she reaches behind to scratch her own back she feels it. She does not feel it at all. For the last 3 days this has escalated and is going faster. She is having difficulty swallowing food now and she cannot actually walk.

PHYSICAL EXAMINATION:

VITAL SIGNS: Blood pressure: 168/90. Temperature: 96.7. Respirations: 24. Heart rate: 104.

GENERAL: She has proximal muscle weakness, both upper and lower extremities. She does have lack of sensation on her back. Her cranial nerves are fully intact at this time. She is unable to lift her arms and her legs due to proximal muscle weakness.

ASSESSMENT AND PLAN:
1. Rapidly progressing neurologic problem: I am going to put her in the hospital for further workup.

Joyce A. Haislip, M.D.
JAH/bdh

My earliest experiences at the OMHS/Owensboro Mercy Health Systems hospital are faint. I think I may have been in emotional shut down. The pain became so intense that I could not focus on anything, but what my body was feeling and it was constant, escalating torment.

The diagnosis is Guillain-Barre Syndrome or GBS. There is not a known cause, not a known, sure treatment, therefore no cure. It can happen to any one, anywhere, at any time and to those of all ages. With first symptoms of GBS the race is on to save a GBS patient's life. It can paralyze the repiratory system. If a person can't breath, then they will die. Many with GBS have lost their lives due to this.

My first day at the hospital was filled with doctors and nurses, tests and uncertainty on my part. I was admitted on Tuesday, January 12th. Swallowing was becoming very difficult, yet I could eat. About mid-day on Wednesday, I felt that familiar tingle, this time in my upper lip and by that evening my face was completely paralyzed. I had no facial expression at all. I was in a daze. Over and over, I ran my hands all over my face. I could feel my touch, yet I could not close my eyes or move my mouth. I tried to raise my brows, but there was nothing... absolutely no response. I am beginning to realize that I am becoming a prisoner in my own body. There are no tears, just the calm of numbness in my brain. I lay there knowing that I am being consumed by this evil thief inside my body, yet inside my brain... I lay in silence. My soul was bent with sadness, yet my brain was numb.

On Thursday Farris and I walked the halls and I felt pretty good. My legs didn't feel any heavier than before and that made me hopeful and happy. We walked several times through the halls. Visitors and patients that we met in the halls smiled and spoke, but I could not smile back, this was the first of a long journey of having a face with no expression.

Of all of my experiences with Guillain-Barre Syndrome, the inability to smile was one of the most difficult losses of this syndrome. I so badly wanted to speak and smile back, but I couldn't smile and my speech was very limited, because I couldn't move my mouth and my tong and vocals were weakened too. This brought an unexplainable sadness.

The next morning was Friday. I asked Farris to help me to the bathroom, by then my legs were weaker than the night before. I needed help walking those few steps to the bathroom. I could take care of my clothing, at that time, but I needed help walking. With each effort to walk, I felt my body succumb to the listlessness that has come to claim my strength. My brain shut down my emotions to this horrific reality. I silently lay and wait for the next test or task of the healthcare workers. I silently lay in wait...

By the time evening came on Friday, I was unable to walk to the bathroom and could not pull myself off of the toilet, nor could I pull my clothes up. By Saturday, I was paralyzed over most of my body. I could move my arms, yet they were very weak. I stared at my legs, concentrating on them with all of my mental energy, demanding them to move, yet there was nothing, absolutely nothing; there was no response at all. How can this be? This bad dream has become a nightmare that I can't escape. I am frozen here and forced to deal with this... but how?...so I numbly lay in silence, bound by this hideous stillness.

My time at the Owensboro Hospital seems like a dream. I didn't have a lot of drugs for pain, yet I have very little recollection of the actual events there. I think my mental defense mechanisms were protecting me from the obvious reality of my situation. Our brains are very complex and have abilities that science only minutely understands. I truly believe that the mental state that I was in at the beginning of GBS was a defense mechanism provided by God. He protected me, so I would not loose me while living through this trauma.

There were so may people praying for my recovery. My name was added to prayer lists in Indiana and Kentucky. I know that God and His son Jesus was with me. He and the helping hands of His Angels cradled my emotions with love and most times with a peaceful calm.

Sissy and I have been friends for about 30 years. Sissy and I were neighbors the first time I lived in Owensboro, Kentucky. We become fast friends and have kept our friendship through the years. She is beautiful, feisty and oh so funny. She was there for me during my cancer... now she is standing next to my bed and I can see concern in her every expression. What a true friendship we have shared over the years. Sissy called her church and placed my name on their prayer list. It is the love and prayers of friends like Sissy that saved me from death's open door.

One of the treatments for GBS is IVIG or immunoglobulin. I was given IVIG fusions for 5 days. After 5 days of infusions my GBS was determined to be resistant to the IVIG and the paralysis continued to quickly take over my body. The doctors consulted with each other and Farris and I, then the decision was made to transfer me to University of Louisville Hospital in Louisville, Kentucky.

Lost

Bewildered by the world I see, a world of unwelcome to the spirit of me.
I turn to walk away, yet footsteps of darkness follows to smother my day.
My days once full of sun, are now darkness each and every one.
I ask you Lord, "deliver me from these hands that are holding me."
My strengths are weakened and have forsaken my peaceful will.
No rest for me, for I walk this valley of darkness still.
"What is the answer Lord, what am I to do? I seek all answers from you."
Another day of unrest, another day I have tried, yet failed my test.
As I lay a bewildered soul, I seek your light to restore my eternal glow.
"Restore the glow of my tired heart, restore me Lord, I am unsure where to start."
Bewildered by the world I see, a world of unwelcome to the spirit of me.
"Oh, spirit of me grieve not, for I will again stand, He will make me whole again."
I search the good of me, no rest 'til I reach that tranquil destiny.
"So, Lord, please take me by the hand, give me strength this day to stand."
I wait on all promises made; I wait and will not falter with Faith.
"Faith, oh Faith, I look to thee, for I know your spirit is carrying me."

Shari Ka, 2004

The decision now is to transfer her for plasmapheresis, and Dr. Shah is in the process of arranging that for us.

DISCHARGE DIAGNOSES
1. Guillain-Barre resistant to IVIG.
2. Hypokalemia.

ally.
my.

axilla.

ALLERGIES
PENICILLIN, IODINE, and MORPHINE.

MEDICATIONS AT DISCHARGE
1. Flexeril 5 mg t.i.d. (she is only taking at bedtime because she has had episodes of urinary incontinence with it).
2. Normal saline at 75 mL/hour.
3. Potassium 30 mEq in 200 mL of normal saline infused slowly 1 run only, may be completed by the time she is transferred.
4. Protonix 40 mg every day.
5. Senna 2 tablets at bedtime.
6. Metamucil 17 grams in 8 ounces of liquid every night.
7. Nitro paste 1 inch for 6 hours for transient hypertension. She does not have it on at this time.
8. Alprazolam 0.25 mg 1/2 tablet twice a day.
9. Isopto Tears 0.5% eye drops p.r.n.
10. Darvocet-N 100, 1-1/2 tablets every 4 hours p.r.n. pain.

DISPOSITION AT DISCHARGE
The patient is poor, and transfer for continued treatment is anticipated today.

JOYCE A HAISLIP, MD

Copy for HAISLIP, JOYCE A, MD

DISCHARGE SUMMARY

NAME: BR   K   ROOM: 4516-01
DOB: 06   PT TYPE:
ATTN PHYS   ISLIP, MD   MR#: 00223588
ADMITTED: ACCT#: 12859464
DISCHARG   MSV: NEU

___

This is _____ patient of mine who presented to my office on the
day of admission complaining of progressive weakness. She initially had
some numbness and tingling in her hands and then that immediately went
to her feet. From her feet it started up her legs to her waist. She
was feeling very strange with her buttocks and also was having
difficulties lifting her arms up over her head, and she was in
significant pain all over. In the office, she demonstrated, she reached
around to her back and actually could not feel her hand touching
herself. This progressed ascendingly very rapidly over the 3 days
prior. The only exposure she had had, she had a sore throat within the
previous week to week and a half that she used some warm salt-water
gargles that resolved it.

She was admitted to the hospital for possible Guillain-Barre. Dr. Shah,
neurology, was consulted immediately. He examined the patient and felt
also that this was a possibility and did a lumbar puncture. There was
no protein elevation in the lumbar puncture which would be expected;
however, because of the rapid progression of this disease he thought
perhaps that was the problem. We did start her on IVIG, and she
received 400 mg/kg daily for 5 days. On day 3, she seemed to have a
significant improvement, strengthening in her lower extremities, but
immediately that was not durable, and she began to become weaker again.
At this point in time, she is now unable to roll over in bed on her own.
She is unable to get up and walk on her own. Her legs are too weak.
She cannot close her lips. She cannot close her eyes. She had some
difficulty with speech. Swallow seems to be intact, but today she feels
that she is not getting as much breath as she was as recent as
yesterday.

She also developed some hypokalemia while here, and that has been fully
repleated. They relate to me now, her husband and the patient, that
last night and yesterday afternoon she was able to actually stand by
herself, but within a couple of hours that was gone, and by midnight she
was back to feeling worse.

Copy for HAISLIP, JOYCE A, MD

Shari Ka

That was January 21, 2010. Dr. Shah and Dr. Haislip wanted to try plasmapheresis, which is the process of removing the blood from the body, separating the blood and the plasma, then replacing the blood so the body can rebuild new plasma and hopefully remove whatever virus or bacteria that has made me sick. Owensboro Mercy Health Systems did not have the machines needed for this procedure. It was also thought that I would get more specialized care for GBS at the University of Louisville Hospital.

I was transported by ambulance from the Owensboro hospital to UofL hospital. The ride was quick and painful. I was bundled in many blankets and pillows to keep me as stationary as possible and to pad the hard surface of the cot. It seemed that we no more than left one hospital, then we were at the next. I don't recall much about being received at the entrance of UofL hospital and only the quick ride through the halls, as I lay motionless on the cot. I could only move my eyes as I scanned the walls and searched the faces of those who were attending to me. I listened to the casual chatter of those passing in the halls. Some of the passers by smiled at me, but I had nothing that I could give back. I lay there motionless, yet there was an ember burning, quietly inside of me. I prayed, "please God, help me through this, I feel so small." I felt the very life of me peacefully, slipping away. I didn't feel panicked, just a calm acceptance, yet there was that ember burning deep inside of me.

My first profound recollection of UofL. is Brina, the nurse that admitted me to UofL. She talked to me the entire time that she was doing the admitting procedures. She talked about how to exercise my face, so I can get my smile back. She showed me the scar on her face from a serious accident and she said it took 3 years to get her smile back. She told me to never give up and Brina, I haven't!! At the time I had not looked into a mirror to see my facial paralysis; therefore I had no idea what I looked like. I knew I couldn't show any expressions, especially to smile. I couldn't close my eyes or speak clearly. I listened with intensity to Brina''s every word, as I studied her every expression and fallowed her with my eyes. At the time the true meanings of her words would not touch me completely. It wasn't until about 2 weeks after I returned home, I looked into the mirror for the first time, and then I knew what Brina was trying so hard to relate to me. I listened with intensity to Brina's every word that day. Brina's words comfort me even today and it has been a year since the beginning of that terrible chapter of my life's journey.

16

Love is…

Love knows not it's self, for it is continually seeking another's needs.

Love is never blind, it is the guiding light through all darkness.

Love is never vain, for it knows only the inner beauty of another.

Love is always first, it does not wait until all else has failed.

Love never slumbers, it is there ever waiting to give.

Love is a guide, to lead to a place of peace.

Love is constant, for it knows no pause.

Love is wise, for it knows all truths.

Love has no limitations, for it knows not time, distance or space.

Love knows not it's self, for it is continually seeking another's needs.

Love is God . . . that yearning in our hearts, to show the world who He is.

Shari Ka, 2004

The neurologist at UofL decided that I should not have the plasmapheresis treatment, because I had been given 5 infusions of immunoglobulin at OMHS. The doctors were concerned that they may remove from my blood any of the benefits of the IVIG infusions that I already had if they performed the blood cleansing of plasmapheresis. The doctors at UofL decided to administer more IVIG infusion. I was given 3 more treatments of the IVIG infusions with hopes that this would stop the progression of GBS and nerve damage.

My time at the University hospital was hard. The nurses were kind, yet with limited power to make things better for me. I look back and realize now that I didn't realize how bad I was. I honestly didn't know. "Oh, thank you God, I didn't know.

I was in CCU for the first 2 weeks. I was unable to sit up, so I couldn't see anything but the ceiling, the walls and those that stood over me. Farris stayed in my room with me day and night. Every day was the same. Pain, drugs, sleep, wake up, pain, drugs, sleep and every few hours a breathing test to check lung capacity and vitals day and night and on and on, it seemed endless.

One of the first tests that I endured was the nerve conduction test. The attendants came for me and took me to the room where the test is done. I silently lay on my cot until it was my turn to be tested. There were patients ahead of me, so I lay there listening to the activities around me. Unfamiliar voices and the busy activities didn't arouse my emotions, which seemed dead inside of me. I lay in motionless silence. It wasn't long before it was my time to have the nerve conduction test. There are 2 electrodes, one placed on each end of the nerve, this measures how quickly the current travels through the nerve. This was absolute agony. The doctors doing the tests were very kind and apologized for the discomfort. I tried so hard to keep from crying out. I didn't cry out, yet I moaned with every electrical charge. The outcome of the test was that the nerves in my legs and feet were devastated. Would I ever walk again?

I could not close my eyes, so I had to have a lubricant in my eyes at all times to keep them from drying out, therefore I was unable to read or watch TV. Louisville had a huge snowstorm while I was there. The morning shift nurse wanted to help me to look out of the window to see the snow, so she raised my bed to allow a perfect view, but I couldn't see any of it. It was at times such as this that I had to face the awareness of my limitations.

There were milestones along the way that brought awareness to me of the peril I was in. One such incident was when the CCU nurse needed to pull me up in bed. I am 5' 8 ½" tall. I am long limbed. I slide down in the hospital beds very easily, especially being a person with paralysis, I had no way to keep myself up in the bed.

I hadn't been at Louisville but a few days when the CCU nurse came to pull me up in bed. She and another nurse were pulling me with the draw sheet, which only came up to my shoulders. When they lifted me, my head dropped down and I could not lift it up. My neck was paralyzed and I could not lift up my head. I didn't realize this until this happened. It was times like this that the seriousness of GBS hit home. It is a helplessness that only those who have experienced it can know.

In the CCU unit I had monitors and wires everywhere. I couldn't swallow, so I had to be suctioned when anything I swallowed wouldn't go down, which was most things I swallowed.

It happened so often that I learned to suction myself. Choking is a very frightening experience!! When your airway is blocked you can feel your heart rate elevate and fight or flight sets in.

With time, I learned to handle the choking and suppress the fight or flight reaction, so I could get through it with the least amount of panic brought on by those psychological and physiological responses.

I was choking on most everything that I swallowed, so a swallowing test was ordered. For the swallowing test, I was placed in a sitting position in front of an x-ray machine. I had to drink liquids of different consistencies. Some liquids were thick and some were thin. This test is to find what consistancy of liquids I could swallow with out the liquids going into my lungs. The test concluded that the paralysis was allowing thin liquids to go to my lungs. This is why I was choking every time I swallowed anything with the consistency of thin liquids. Aside from the discomfort of getting liquids into the lungs, this can cause pneumonia.

One of the side effects of the nerve damage was that I had an unquenchable thirst. My mouth was always dry and I craved water my every waking minute. I was put on a diet of thick liquids, because thin liquids, such as water and the like would go directly to my lungs. Thin liquids are water or any substance with the same consistency as water. Thick water is the most horrific liquid ever made. Thick water is water base with a cornstarch like substance in it. I tried so hard to drink it, but I couldn't get it to stay down, it was awful!! I could have orange juice, which I drank as much as I could get to avoid the thick water and to keep hydrated.

The first time my son, Daniel came to CCU to see me, it was very difficult for him. My son has only known me to be athletic. A person strong, fit and full of energy that never stops. It hurt for him to see me like this. He cried and I so badly wanted to comfort him, yet there was nothing I could do. I had many visitors and nearly everyone was tearful. I tried so hard to be me, but this was one time I couldn't pull it off. I was me, but I wasn't.

Cameron and his fiancé Brooke, came and sat by my bed as I drifted in and out of sleep. I was thinking that I need to stay awake to visit with them. They drove from Indianapolis to Louisville several times and stayed for hours, but I couldn't stay awake during their visits. This was the routine every time I had visitors. I could manage a few minutes of lucidness here and there, then I would drift off to sleep or at best I was too lethargic to respond to their conversations. Although I was not good company, it was wonderful to see those who came to visit me. It meant so much to me to have loved ones near. Their visits offered Farris a much-needed break too. Most of the time he and the guests would go to the cafeteria. This gave Farris time away from me and our seemingly endless routine.

By now the pain from the nerve damage was so horrendous that I could not realize anything, but it's constant torment. The sensory nerves are for the sensation of touch. My sensory nerves had been severely damaged and the nerve messages had gone acutely array. My skin felt as if it was literally on fire. There is not one word or group of words that can truly describe the intensity of this pain. It is as if the entire body has been severely burned. If one is held in boiling oil non-stop, this is the torment of what GBS nerve pain is like. The slightest touch from my sheets, the torment of my body lying in my bed, the agony when health care workers had to handle my body brought pain unimaginable. I am a reserved person, yet with the slightest touch on my skin, I screamed in pain. Mentally I could not withstand the constant, unrelenting torture. The pain medicines were my only salvation. I received an injection every 6 hours. That pain medicine lasted about 4 hours, which meant I had about 2 hours of absolute torture, which felt like an eternity. Every minute after the pain medications had worn off, I cried and begged the nurses to help me. I yearned for the nothingness of unconscious sleep.

Farris's sisters came to Louisville from Lafayette, Indiana to see me. It was at the time when the pain was at it's worse. The slightest touch was agony. Carrie and Amie are twins and the sweetest people. While they were there I had to be turned, which meant torturous pain and I cried out. I could see their tears. I tried so hard to contain the agony, but I couldn't. I wanted to comfort them and tell them it was o-k, but I couldn't. With every movement and touch, I lost the battle to block-out the pain.

There came a time when the progression of the paralysis had stopped and the danger of paralysis taking over my diaphragm and lungs had passed, so I was moved to a two-bed room. Farris had a smaller cot to sleep on and there was much less chance of getting rest. It seemed that each day and each week just ran together for me. I was so involved with my pain that I couldn't concentrate on anything else. I just want it to go away. I wanted anything that would help me sleep, so I wouldn't have to deal with the pain.

My feet began to contract, which is a very serious condition caused by paralysis. The tendons began to contract and to draw up, which was making my feet stiffen in a straight out position without the ability to flex them. I have seen folks that have paralysis with this condition.

I was so surprised that it happens so quickly. The doctors ordered a boot for me to wear, which helped to keep my feet flexed and from becoming fixed with the shortened tendons. The doctor explained to me, if this happens, the only thing to correct it is surgery and sometimes that type of surgery is not successful. This frightened me, because this could prevent me from walking again or at best I could not walk normal again. This condition is seen a lot with those who have cerebral pulsey

While I was in the two-bed room, I met a wonderful family. Candy, Bob and their son, Trev. Candy has cancer and the news was not good. She was in my room for about a week or so. I became acquainted with Candy, as we talked back and forth through the curtain that was pulled most of the time. She is a person that I will never forget. Candy and her family are just precious. She and her husband watched out for me if I needed anything when Farris stepped out of the room. They became acquainted with Farris and Daniel. We exchange Christmas cards and have talked on the phone a couple of times. I will always consider those wonderful people as friends. Most of the other patients that were in my room after Candy left, were only there a day or two, then was moved to a different room or they were discharged.

Farris stayed by my side night and day and it was taking its toll on him. He looked as if he was a walking dead man. I had to be turned every two hours and Farris got very good at knowing exactly where to place each of the pillows and how to move each limb. I had to have pillows under and against my back to keep me on my side each time I was turned. When a person is paralyzed they are unable to keep themselves up while lying on their side. With out the supports, I would just fall back over onto my back. He knew how to pull the draw sheets in a way to cause the least amount of pain. He changed my boot every 2 hours. He tried to sleep in the tiny cot next to my bed while I was sleeping; yet he rarely got comfortable enough for restful sleep.

Farris was experiencing burn out and went home for 3 days. While he was gone, I had a nurse that had worked in the burn unit. She turned me and moved me in a way that caused minimal discomfort. She knew exactly how to handle my body, which caused little intrusion to my damaged nerves.

If I could instruct health care providers with instructions that would be helpful to patients with GBS or like conditions, it would be to handle them as if they are burn patients. A GBS patient has the same sensation as a person that has been burned; therefore it only makes sense to handle them as a burned patient.

I had wonderful nurses and techs to care for me. Of course, as it is in any profession, there were some better than others, yet most all of the health professionals that I encountered during my hospital stay were wonderful. Of course there will be a few that will always have a special place in my heart. Those that touched me the most are those that cared, I mean truly cared. A patient feels the difference from a health care worker who is just mechanically doing a job and one who shows true compassion with their professionalism. I will never forget each of those wonderful people.

The days begin to run together. Pain medicines. sleep, then awake in pain knowing I have to wait for more meds and the agony of that wait. I came to a low point when I felt I couldn't bare the endless, unrelenting agony any longer. I wanted God to relieve my pain by letting me die. I told no one this, but I wanted to be free of the pain so much that I was ready for the peace of heaven's eternity. I had no fear, just the need to be free of the constant, unbearable torment.

I Am Still Me

When daylight comes, as daylight will, I see… I know this stillness, relentlessly come to claim the all of me, the all of me, this silent will in stillness cannot be, surely this stillness… surely this stillness is not me.

I lay in remembrance of yesterday's exuberance. A time of new gain and fun, a time I run to life's mysteries undone. A time oft with out a care. A time to dream, a time I dare. A time of life's songs a whispering, each note in wait of hope's caress. A time of life's songs, yet unsung. A place to be, a place to sing, this place does dwell anticipation's happiness.

Today a body lay in wait, a wait no person, place or thing can penetrate. The answers locked away, they are not to be given up to rescue me today. The answers hide in secret's dismay; the answers lay in stillness locked away.

Ah, come hither morning's beckoning light, I reach to somewhere and gather me; I cry out to call again the me I used to be. Ah, at morning's early light I rudely withstand my awakening. The me I used to be, yes, I rudely awaken me. Ah there… awakens the me I used to be.

Oh stillness you I boldly fight; I wilt not wait for daylights dreams to wake. I boldly fight… 'tis I to turn from slumber's place. This body cannot stay in slumber's, cold and silent place. No place for me to stay in slumber's place.

When daylight comes, as daylight will, I see dawn's newness near. I see dawn's sunlight bright, my soul does earnestly endear. My world all new… reborn from memories wills. All mysteries reveal where newness slept. Awaken… go and sing all songs unsung, no longer held in quiet stills. This new day, it must be won.

Ah, the best of me is me, the best of me is me. Not stillness, nor daydreams, nor memories past, not anything of now that silently lay. It is me, I am still me… the best of me is not what you see… the best of me is the heart of me… the best of me is me.

By: Shari Ka, GBS, 2010

On one of those days that I felt I could no longer withstand this burning agony, I used my cell phone to call Dr. Haislip. I think I just wanted to hear the reassuring, familiar friendliness in her voice. I got her answering service. I think it was on a Sunday, yet I didn't know one day from another. She called right back and all I could do was cry. I told her that I was afraid. I was... I was afraid of having to live out my life with this pain and I knew that I couldn't do it. I don't recall what she said to me, but what ever it was, I calmed down.

Try to imagine being a healthy, physically fit individual one-day... literally, then looking at your body and being unable to move... being paralyzed. Never in my farthest imagination have I ever thought this could or would happen to me. I am physically strong for a woman. I love gardening; mowing, landscaping, long walks in the woods and all the activities an energetic person enjoys. Everyday consisted of creating a new project and the wonderful challenge to get it done. I have always loved physical challenges. Those activities that make you push your every physical ability. I love life and the freedom of a healthy body to pursue anything that came to mind... and most days this is what I did.

The doctors were trying different formulas of pain medications and doing as much as they could to provide me with some relief from the agony, yet I now know that there was probably not a magical formula that would take the pain completely away from me. The only escape for me was to sleep. For the first time in my life, I yearned to succumb to sleep. My every waking minute was consumed with the desire to escape into the unawareness of sleep.

One of my nurses on the evening shift was Sam. Sam was so funny. He made me laugh, although I had no facial expressions, I laughed from my heart. I really did!! On the first evening that Sam was my nurse, he was upbeat and smiling. He told me a joke. I smiled, yet with a paralyzed face there was no expression, even I forgot at that moment, because his joke was funny!!

The next evening Sam came into my room and was doing something for me, I don't recall what... he told another joke and I was smiling...on the inside, because the joke was funny. Sam said to me, "Mrs. Bradford, you can smile anytime" and something about his jokes not being that bad. I replied, "Sam, I am laughing at your joke, my face is paralyzed and I can't smile!!"

Sam was so embarrassed and kept apologizing to me and I think that was the funniest part of the entire joke. He felt so bad, yet the situation was funnier to me than his joke. I still get a good laugh from it!! That was my first time to know it is o-k that I can't smile outwardly, because I am still me inside and smiling just as I always have. Sam was one of the best nurses at the hospital.

One evening my tech mentioned something about my oxygen level getting lower. I didn't take what he was saying seriously, because I was so sleepy. He came in 2 times to check it and seemed very concerned. Not only did I go to sleep... I stopped breathing. This is why the tech was so concerned that my oxygen level was dropping. The next thing I recall was a nurse who was shaking me and shouting at me to wake up.

I was looking at her through my mental haze and I knew what had happened. The room was filled with people and every kind of monitor. I had the loudest sounds in my head, as if someone was blowing air directly into my ears. I was thinking that they had turned my oxygen up all of the way and it was making these loud sounds in my head. I knew that things had gone terribly wrong.

The nurse asked me if I recognized my husband and I did, she asked me to say his name and I did, she asked me to point him out and I did, he was standing across the room with the Chaplain. The nurse asked me if I knew what happened. I knew that I had too much pain medicine, which is what had happened.

The doctors had called in a group of Pain Specialist to assist them with a plan for my pain management. They were trying different formulas of drugs to help control my pain and ready me for my transition to go home.

My body cannot tolerate most medications. I can plan on some kind of side affects from foreign chemicals when ingested into my body. Before going to the hospital with GBS the only medicine I ever took was an occasional Excedrin or an aspirin.

My tolerance level is very low to dosages of drugs. A normal dose for most people would be half that amount for me. Many times when I have taken prescription drugs, I take half the amount recommended and that is usually the correct dosage for me.

The Chaplain asked for us to pray together. Farris, the Chaplain and I prayed together. I saw J, my tech and Tina, my nurse working with the other nurses and it was a beehive of activity. J asked Farris to come to the head of the bed and hold my hand and as soon as Farris stood next to me, I was out again. I briefly awoke again and the wonderful nurse that had been shouting at me to wake up was still there... there was something in her voice that was comforting to me, then I fell asleep again, I awoke again for a few seconds and I heard her say something about how everything is going o-k now. I awoke again the next morning around 7:00 a.m., with all of the monitors still attached to me. I had an oxygen monitor on my finger and one on my toe and every time I didn't breath as I should the monitor beeped, which meant it beeped every few minutes. I still had the loud sound of air rushing through my ears. It took the rest of the day for that sensation and sound to leave.

At the time, I think I was really upset with some of the doctors. Most of the doctors were really good doctors and they showed genuine interest and care concerning my recovery and real compassion for me. I had many doctors visiting me every day. This is a University Hospital and many of the medical students are assigned to patient care, as well as many others observe and learn from a patient's illness. One doctor in particular, while on his morning rounds and accompanied by his students, said to his students, "in his opinion my outcome didn't look good. He said that I might not walk again, because my nerves were devastated." As I lay there listening to this, I vowed to myself I would prove him wrong.

While talking with one of the doctors, he said that if I ever walked again it would be 2 to 3 years. I told him, "that he just didn't know me and I would walk before that." He was kind and trying to prepare me for what was a head. I wouldn't allow those negatives to penetrate my optimism. I wouldn't hear of any of it.

I had faith that God would heal me enough that I could walk again and of this I had no doubts. As I look back on all of the events I lived through, it was a blessing that I truly wasn't aware of how serious my condition really was. If I had known, I may not have been so sure of myself, yet I believe that I was spared that knowledge, so I could maintain my determined optimism. God was carrying me.

As The Butterflies Dance

I wind the road, through trees and hills. A heavy heart with saddened will. No light to feel, to see, no light of day to brighten the darkness of me…, then magic, as magic will, that moment my world stood still, as I turn the last bend I see, a wonderment awaiting me, a wonderment to erase all cares, a heavenly sight awaiting there.

My soul felt joy with the welcoming sight of the butterflies dancing in luminous sunlight. Flowers reaching to sunlight's call, embracing each butterfly, as they glide by. Surely Angels and rainbows orchestrated this colorful gift. I stand in awe at this sight, the butterflies skip and soar to nature's harmony, this greeting I know was meant just for me. A loveliness that only God could make, ah, a butterfly dance, just for my sake.

Butterflies moving with silent grace to compositions of Angels songs. I stand in awe as my soul can hear beyond the silence, the cords and notes as the butterflies dance. Each note an awareness comes to say, I have been away too long. With each breath of wind, the butterflies glide in performance surely Angel's guide. The butterflies dance a language of softened strength, spoken with each dip and soar, a message I will always hold dear, I have been away too long, I have been away too long, this I hear, I feel and know as the butterflies dance a welcome for me…, I have been away too long, too long… in awe is my stance… as the butterflies dance.

By: Shari Ka, 2004

It wasn't long after that I was ready to leave the hospital. The doctors tried their best to encourage/persuade me to agree to go to a rehab. center before returning home. At this point I was unable to pull myself up in bed or to sit up. The doctors were very concerned about sending me home in the condition that I was in.

At the time of my discharge from UofL, I was paralyzed with the exception of my arms and hands. Although there was a great deal of weakness in my arms and hands, I had no restrictions of their use. By then I could hold my head up, and that felt wonderful!! My earnest hopes and prayers were that I could learn to sit up on my own power. I didn't ask for or hope for anything past that at that time. The old saying, "one day at a time" suddenly, I was realizing and living its true meaning.

The day had arrived and I was going home!!! It was February 14th, Valentines Day!! That morning the nurses and Social Worker were busy getting all of my paper work done with all of the last minute instructions for home care.

It seemed it took forever, although they worked very efficiently and with great care. Then the news came that the transport ambulance had arrived and the attendants would be up to get me soon. There they were, two attendants with a gurney to take me home!! They placed me on the gurney and down the hall I went heading towards the elevator.

As I passed the nurses station, I thanked everyone and waved good-bye. What a wonderful feeling that was!! The doors of the hospital opened and I felt the cold air in my face and I loved it! I took a deep breath with absolute joy. The attendants loaded me into the ambulance and off we went.

Both the driver and the young lady that was monitoring my vitals were Paramedics. They made my ride home very comfortable as we engaged into some very interesting conversations. I relayed to them that my daughter is a Paramedic and they seemed very interested in learning about her job working at the Fire Dept.

It is around a 3 ½ hour drive from Louisville to Lafayette, yet it seemed to take only minutes. Farris had gone ahead of us to be sure that everything was ready for my arrival. The driver got lost and it was growing dark, as it gets dark early in the winter. I tried to give him directions, yet I didn't realize how difficult that would be while laying, strapped down on a cot.

I had them to turn onto Rd. 350, which would have taken us nearly to my home, yet I told them to turn the wrong way on Rd. 350. They decided to go by their GPS and not a lady lying down, unable to see much more than the ceiling of the ambulance. They found their way through Purdue University campus and right to my driveway, where Farris was waiting to guide them up the long driveway to our house.

The attendants brought me through the garage and into the breakfast area of my kitchen, which is where my hospital bed had been set up. It was nice, because I could see out of the french doors and into the back yard.

The first thing that I noticed was the smell of my home. It was magnificent!! For the first time, I could smell familiarity. I looked all around me and there were my wall hangings, the decorating that I had so carefully done when we moved into our home, it was all so welcoming, although my face was paralyzed, I had a smile that I could not stop!! I felt that smile to the depths of my soul.

I have 3 dogs and the entire time that I was in the hospital, they were in my thoughts. I yearned to hold them and feel the way they used to snuggle up on my lap. Molli is my German Shepherd. I adopted her from Crystal Creek Kennels. She had been a stray and was obviously in need of love. She is so sweet and beautiful and I know she was watching for me every day, because she has always followed me everywhere. Jami is a Shi Tzu and a bundle of joy. He is the sweetest, lap dog. Every time I sit down, he is in my lap. He has bright, blue, loving eyes. Then there is Ami, she is a Bishon Frisse'. She is dainty and oh so cute. She looks just like the prissy, little girl that she is. It was so wonderful to touch them and hold them again!! When Marilyn first put them on my bed, they seemed afraid and it hurt a little, yet I knew that they would come around when things calmed down a little and I was right. After about a week, Jami wanted to lay on the bed with me and it is amazing how comforting having his sweet little body next to me was.

Some of my family were there waiting for me... My sister Marilyn, came to stay with us to help with my daily care, my niece Kelley who is a Massage Therapist and also is a trained physical therapy assistant and Kelley's daughter, Harley.

Kelley was to be my physical therapist. She applied message therapy with my daily physical therapy routine. This combination gave me a kick-start to my recovery. I highly recommend physical therapy combined with message therapy for a more successful outcome of recovery for conditions involving paralysis. The massage therapy helps with the loss of circulation one has due to nerve damage.

I was so happy to see everyone!! I then noticed the most beautiful bouquet of pink carnations, daisies and babies breath on the bar. It was huge and so beautiful!! I could smell the fragrance of the flowers from across the room. Our neighbors and friends, Joe and Joy Erwin made sure that the flowers were there to welcome me home. It is true; flowers say I love you in a very special way!!

About an hour after I had gotten home and settled, Marilyn and I were just talking about what to have for dinner. For the first time in weeks, I was starving. Just as we started questioning

29

what to eat there was a knock on the door. It was Joe and Joy. Joy had made some broccoli soup for us. They brought other things with it, but the smell of that soup was heavenly. We all laughed at their timing. They visited for a few minutes. Joe offered a beautiful prayer as we all joined hands, then they left us to enjoy our feast. The soup was so delicious! To my surprise and everyone else's, I had seconds. To this day it is my favorite!!

Marilyn and Farris had a strict schedule of medications for me. I took pills every 4 and 6 hours around the clock, which meant that someone had to get up in the night to be sure I had my meds. After awhile, Marilyn and Farris took turns as to who would get up in the night.

At night meds. were due at 11:00 pm, 3:00 am, then another due at 7:00 am. On the nights that Marilyn administered the meds, she and I would stay up until my 3:00 am meds. were taken, then we fell asleep.

We spent a lot of time talking during those late night hours. It was tiring for both of us, yet I will always love that memory of those late night visits.

Kelley started working with me the day after I got home. She started with range of motion in my hips and back. In the beginning of the ROM routine, I was lying there thinking… those gentle rotations of my limbs surely are not going to help much. I never let on the doubts that I had, because I knew Kelley knew what she was doing.

I so badly wanted to sit up on my own and she said that I would before I knew it. I wasn't as optimistic, yet I had so much hope and a powerful determination. All I knew is that I did not want to be like this the rest of my life and I was going to do everything I needed to do to get me back.

At the hospital the physical therapists came about 3 times and tried to force my body to sit up with their assistance. The pain was so excruciating that I couldn't do it. At one point, I did get to a sitting position; they tried to help me stand, which of course was useless, because my legs were completely paralyzed. They wanted to get me up and sitting in a chair next to my bed, before they released from the hospital. The pain was so unbearable, that I refused to allow them to try after the second attempt.

Kelley explained that I needed to have a routine of range of motion or ROM's in my joints, before I would be ready to sit up. After a couple of weeks of the ROM's, Kelley announced that I was ready to sit up. I was terrified with the thought of experiencing the same pain that I had felt while in the hospital, so I didn't think I could do it. She and Farris gently eased me forward and to my surprise there was very little discomfort. Finally!!!! I was sitting up!! It seemed that once I accomplished that everything else started waking up in my body.

Next Kelley wanted me to try to stand. I was so afraid of falling. Farris and Kelley wedged themselves against my body and slowly helped me stand. My legs would not hold me, yet they supported me enough to allow my feet to apply pressure on the floor. There are no words to explain how good it felt to feel the cool tile on the bottoms of my feet

The first thing I noticed as I stood there is that I am tall. I have never had a reason to notice how tall I am, until the first time I stood up next to Kelley and Farris. I was so surprised!! We all had a laugh out of that!!

Now that I am sitting up on my own, I wanted to sit in a chair alone, so Kelley and Farris put a chair next to my bed and I started sitting up in a chair. Each day, I stayed in the chair longer. How sweet it is!! My prayer was answered. The one thing I so badly wanted to do, I am doing it!! I started sitting in the chair to eat all of my meals and that was another piece of heaven!! It is hard to explain how wonderful a feeling it is to be able to sit in a chair, unassisted and enjoy a meal.

Change

Change brings new dreams, pursuits of untouched promises: treasures of the heart only imaginations knew. Change is offerings: offerings of possibilities true.

Change... be it a wish, a challenge, an unexpected turn, an unsettling force, a pause in time, a change of course: seemingly a thief that interrupted you.

Change... oft a stranger disrupting tranquil slumber: awakening one from silent stills: a quiet wedge of walls, which threatens a solid will.

What ever is or brings about: if hope or enemy unannounced: change serves truths with elements of time. Change brings time's wisdom and blessings to thine.

Change brings new dreams and pursuits of untouched promises: treasures of the heart only imaginations knew. Change is offerings: offerings of possibilities...possibilities just for me and you.

Shari Ka, 2000

Joy brought a little apparatus like a small bicycle. It is meant to exercise feet and legs. It sat very low on the floor and she wanted to know if I would like to try it. I was very eager to try and to everyone's amazement, mine including, I could do it, not well mind you, but the fact that I could do it at all was amazing!! I had very little control of the movements of my legs, yet just enough that I could move those peddles around. It seemed once I got started it was hard for me to stop. It was a new freedom that I had lost weeks ago; it was a light of hope. As my legs flopped back and forth, I slowly and unsteadily peddled away.

Kelley's plan was to assign me exercises to do in between her visits, which were daily. I worked so hard. At first I wasn't sure how much use I would get back in my legs. When I came home from the hospital, I was emaciated. I was literally a skeleton with skin on it. When they lifted my legs, my muscles, or what was left of them, literally hung down with very little form. My calf muscles had no tone at all. I had lost muscle tone over all of my body. I had a long hard road of recovery ahead of me, yet seeing the poor shape that I was in only made me more determined to get me back.

Since I was admitted to the hospital January 12th, I had not looked into a mirror. I am not sure why, but the opportunity or desire never came up. I didn't feel curious, because I didn't realize that my face had changed so much. It was time for me to have a look at my face. I honestly didn't expect that I looked much different than I always had.

I was handed the mirror and I was shocked by the face looking back at me. There was very little resemblance to the person I was before Guillain-Barre Syndrome. My face had literally dropped down. My lower eyelids were drooping down and lying away from my eyeballs. My face looked like a mask. I thought to myself, this is what everyone had been looking at that cared for me and visited me? It must have been a shock to my visitors too. I told myself right then, this is the least of your worries… I want to stand and hopefully walk; I will be concerned about the appearance of my face later.

I was so proud when I learned to scoot myself in the bed. My legs began to slowly move to my commands. The ability to move them myself was such a triumphant time of my recovery. This healing process sometimes seemed painfully slow, yet there are no words to explain the joy of these small, yet emotionally, enormous successes!! The most wonderful success is when I began to roll myself over, sit up and bend down to change my boot.

Some of the things I had to learn again were things one would never imagine. I had to learn to yawn and belch again. I had to learn to pee again. For months I had to use a catheter, because my bladder was paralyzed. It was a long time before I could put a straw into my mouth and suck it. My mouth would not close, so I had to hold my lips closed with my fingers pinched around a straw in order to drink. It was the same with eating. I had to hold my mouth closed by pinching my lips closed, so I could retain the food that was in my mouth. The left side of my mouth would not close and I drooled constantly. I had to deal with the humiliation of not having any control over my bowels. I couldn't feel when they were going to move. I was void of any of the sensations a body has to let you know of needed body functions. Everything was gone. When I came home from the hospital, I had less physical abilities than a newborn baby.

The days turned into weeks. I was sitting up on the side of the bed with no help. I was washing my own hair, in bed with Marilyn and Farris's help. Marilyn soon began putting everything I needed for bathing and grooming in a container and placed it on my bed and turned me loose!!

How wonderful it was to be able to bath myself and change my boot every 2 hours. I could actually bend forward enough to change my boot!! That was a proud accomplishment!! I was enjoying and relishing in my new independence. Nothing was easy, yet I decided that GBS wasn't going to be who I am.

Kelley thought it was time to use the walker to try to stand. I loved the idea of standing and I passed with flying colors. After a few times of standing, next was to take a step of two, I did it!! My legs were starting to wake up a little and I could shuffle them into stepping motions enough that I could make a few steps. It seemed from that day forward, I began to get some strength back in my legs. A few steps then a few more around the bar in the kitchen. I hated the walker, because it was such a slow process. Step, and then push the walker forward with the same routine again and again.

More days and weeks went by and it was time for Kelley to allow me to take over most of my strengthening exercises and ROM's. She was very pleased with my progress and so was I.

Things Temporary

Yonder stand on distant hill, daylight's fading guide, 'tis gone and I find not my course, this course my gloom does hide. Oh, darkness fill me full, 'tis sadness come to stay? 'tis sadness one more day. I look about my room, no light of heart in me, no light of heart in me. I search the open skies, I walk to pattern's song, Oh, pattern all day long. I search at least a vacant smile, none for me I see, none for me I see. 'tis sadness come to stay? 'tis sadness one more day. My soul with weakened plea, a plea for life... now hidden from me, no will of good do I see. Each new day begins, yet I, not a part of it, I am not a part of it. My will took pause in time, my will is no longer mine, it seems... no longer mine it seems.

Yonder stand on distant hill, the light, the guide of me. Oh, whisper of light, 'tis beckoning me. A flicker deep inside, so faint and sure to hide, so faint and wants to hide. 'tis hope a calling me, 'tis hope in shadows of my gloom, 'tis hope a calling me, 'tis hope I faintly see, 'tis hope still beckoning me. I turn to question still, to doubt, to turn away... in my plea of despair... I know no one is there, no one is there to really care, yet in dimness of light I stand with all my weakened strength, I lift my eyes to see, 'tis hope there for me? Is hope really there for me?

Standing at my door, 'tis hope once more. I grasp the light of it, so sure to slip away, so sure it will not stay. In desperation's call, I reach with weakened heart, I reach with all of me, 'tis hope I dimly see, 'tis hope to rescue me? 'tis hope to rescue me. A message forcing through the darkness of this room, this message I could not see, I could not hear, this message ever near. 'tis hope a standing there, 'tis hope was always there. Hope I could not see, for darkness hides my day, yet hope's enduring song, no thing to change it's stay. 'tis hope a telling me, all sadness and gloom... 'tis things temporary... no longer to keep a heart in distant, darkened room, for sadness and gloom, with God's hope... 'tis things temporary.

By: Shari Ka, 2005

It was time for Marilyn to go home. She wasn't getting the rest that she needed and I was ready to take on the tasks that she had been doing for me. I hated to see her go, because she had been a very dependable crutch and great company for me, yet I knew it was time. I was apprehensive about being without her, but I didn't let it show. If I had let her know, she would have stayed, so I said nothing. It was one more step to becoming independent, yes it was time.

After the weather warmed up, I asked Farris if he would put me in the wheel chair and take me walking outside and he didn't think it was a good idea. He told me I didn't need to be outside. I so badly wanted to see something besides these walls. I wanted to go out side and smell the air. I felt very helpless at that point, as I lay in the bed and entertain the negative what ifs. What if I had to depend on others the rest of my life, just to go outside? The thought was devastating, yet it gave me a will to fight like I have never known.

Crystal is a wonderful friend of ours and she came by a lot. She manicured my nails and toes and combed my hair. She would come by and say, "tell me, Shari, what is it you would like to do or have done for you today?" She was a true, caring friend!! This particular day, I asked her if she would put me in the wheel chair and take me a walk out side. She was delighted!! She bundled me up and away we went.

She pushed me up and down the road until I was ready to go in. I will never forget how good it felt to be outside for the first time!! Crystal took me walking in the wheel chair a couple of times; it was such a boost to my esteem to look up and see the endless sky and the beautiful clouds. The cool air felt so refreshing, oh how I missed this simple freedom!!

Some time in April Crystal came by and asked if I was ready to get into the shower. I was so excited!! She put my potty chair, which I was no longer using, in my shower and that is what I sat on. She bought a flexible shower hose, so I could bath myself. How absolutely wonderful to feel the warm water washing over my body!! A shower!! I sat there as if I was just handed a gift from heaven. It is amazing how something so simple can bring such sheer pleasure and joy. One more freedom, yes, I earned one more freedom!!

It was somewhat embarrassing to have others see me and my poor wasted body, yet I think it is something folks like myself get past and realize that we must forfeit our modesty for at least a little while. You are never fully comfortable with the lack of privacy, yet what other options do you have? You get this realization early on.

Crystal was always there. When I first came home, I had no TV were my bed was, so Crystal brought a CD player and books on CD's for me to listen to. I can't tell you what that meant to me. I lay in my hospital bed listening to the stories and it took me away from my new reality. It was relaxing and emotionally therapeutic to escape into the lives of the characters in the stories. Marilyn and I both enjoyed listening to those stories together.

As time went on, I became stronger, although balance was my biggest enemy. I arrived at the place where I had the strength in my legs to stand unassisted; yet I could not keep my balance.

When Farris would go out side, I started sliding out of the bed and hold onto the bar and walk around it. I didn't let him know. Many times I needed a glass of water or something to eat, so I would slip off of the bed, use the walker to get to what I needed and shuffle and slide one step at a time to go back to the bed. It was a struggle to do anything, but I so badly wanted to be able to do for myself again. I know that I took some dangerous chances, but I couldn't just lay in that bed and wait.

I did this every day. There were a few times, I wasn't sure I was going to make it back to the bed, yet I told myself that if plan A fails, then I will go to plan B, which was to slide down on my butt, then scoot back and pull myself up. Thank you, Lord, I never had to use plan B.

One evening Farris came in from working outside, I had a surprise for him. I walked down the hall without the walker. I was so proud of my success. I held my hands out to steady my balance and the way I waddled!! What a wonderful new found freedom!! I now know exactly what it feels like to be a toddler again. I mean that with all seriousness. I now know why toddlers hold out there arms and walk bow legged. It is to keep balance. This is exactly how I relearned to walk. It was a struggle and it was very frightening at times, yet the freedom of being able to take one step after another was the same sensation if one could take off and fly. When I see a toddler struggling to walk, I know their joys and fears.

Farris would go out side every day and I would lie in the bed so badly wanting to go out side. One sunny, spring day, I decided I would go outside by my own power. I got my walker to the front door. I got the door open and the walker on the porch, but the real challenge was to get down the steps that the walker didn't fit on. I was really worried about that. I was afraid of falling, because I was still very unsteady and one slip and I could get seriously hurt; yet I wanted out of the house so badly. It was getting so pretty out and it was warm.

My soul yearned to be outside. I made it!! Farris was at the pond, which is at the bend in the driveway. He seemed shocked to see me. I was very unstable and wasn't sure I should be doing this with no help, but I was determined to get out and enjoy the spring air.

After that, getting myself out side became a daily routine. My first walk with out the walker was quite a chore, but I was determined!! We have a very long driveway and a long walk to the mailbox.

On another inviting, sunny day I decided that my goal for the day was to walk unassisted to the mailbox!! I started out with no walker for the first time. I was so unsteady, yet I went very slow and stopped to rest along the way. What would normally be about a 3-minute walk took at least 20 minutes, but I did it!! I was nervous, because my balance was so unsteady, yet, I did it!! I waited for about 3 weeks before I tried it again. I am stubborn to the point of recklessness and I knew I was pushing too hard and it could be dangerous.

One day I walked outside and asked Farris if I could help him pick up the rocks on the banks of the pond. Farris was picking up all of the small rocks in preparation to sow grass seed. I got a chair and tried sitting in the chair as I picked up the rocks. It was one of those defining moments when you know; you just aren't able to do this. It was hard to realize that I wasn't strong enough to pick up even a few little rocks. I didn't feel discouraged or defeated; just that awareness of my paralysis, yet more determined that I will do this, maybe not today, but I will in time.

Every day was a struggle to accomplish the most basic tasks. I didn't feel discouraged, or ever thoughts of giving up. I did feel a great joy with any new thing I could do, such as bathing myself, getting food and water for myself, using my own bathroom again, sleeping in my own bed again. The things that we all take for granted everyday. The things that we give little or no thought to, unless that freedom has been taken away, then those simple tasks become one's primary focus and hopefully a triumph everyday.

What new thing will I be able to work on and earn back today? Mentally my focus was on the most basic things, as a small child learning to master the immediate world around it.

I usually sent Farris to do the shopping, because I didn't want to be in the public eye. Most of my face was still paralyzed and with that my lower eyelids were drooping all the way down. In a way, I looked like a monster. My eyes were always dry and burning, because I still could not close them.

The left eye would not close at all and the right eye would close a little more than half way. I had to use an eye ointment in my eyes to keep them lubricated, which would ooze onto my cheeks and add to the oddness of this odd looking woman's face.

At this time I was o-k with my outward appearance, I just don't like to be the center of attention, I never did. My comfort zone is to be the wallflower. I tried to stay out of the public as much as I could. When we went for an outing or shopping, I would ride along with Farris, but stay in the car.

There came a time when I felt like testing the waters, so to speak. I wanted to go shopping with Farris. I went to the BMV to get a handicap tag, so we could park near the doors at shopping centers. As I was waiting my turn at the BMV, a disabled veteran struck up a conversation with me, relating the details of his disabilities. He was wounded in Vietnam. I thought to myself, that makes sense that he is here getting his handicap tag, yet why am I here? Sometimes my new life struggles and challenges seemed as if, surely this is a dream. What am I doing here… how can this be?

I decided while in public to keep my sunglasses on and cover my catheter bag well, especially in the closeness of the stores, then no one would be spooked by the sight of my drooping eyelids, blood shot and weeping eyes. This was the answer. Such a simple solution gave me a very welcome freedom. Farris would go into the store and bring out a wheel chair, grocery cart combination. He would push it to a place that I could manage getting from the car to the wheel chair. I had to swing my legs out of the car, then hold onto the chair as I stood, swing my body around to plop into the seat of the chair, then with my hands pick up my legs and adjust my feet to fit the foot supports. I had to lift my legs with my hands, because there was not enough strength in my legs to enable me to lift them up without help. After we got into the store, up and down the isles we would go. The only problem was… I pretty much knew where everything was in the store and he didn't. Farris is hard of hearing and my speech was very limited and my voice was hardly audible. After a while, I just handed him the note and pointed. Were we ever a sight!!

The wheel chair was a symbol of helplessness to me. Of all of the mechanics I had to depend on, the wheel chair, I hated. It attracted attention everywhere I went, but most difficult, was the awareness of the limited control of my body. I was in that chair being pushed, because I couldn't walk.

It was in the wheel chair that I had to face my reality. My legs were nearly useless. How can that be? I was determined to become strong enough that I would not have to use that wheel chair again.

The grocery store had an electric shopping cart and several times Farris encouraged me to try it. I felt intimidated by it and of course it was symbol of helplessness, which I loathed. Finally, at his urging I decided to try it.

I got in the cart and felt a little clumsy at first. I learned very quickly how to operate it and away I went. I sent Farris one-way and I would go another. It was amazing the freedom that I felt. I really didn't pay much attention to the looks I was getting. I felt like Mario Andredi!! When the carts are fully charged they have a lot of speed. I have to admit, it was fun!! The cart was one more step forward for me. I have a new and greater respect for those who must depend on these mechanical devices. They permit freedom for those who would not have the ability to do basic chores, such as shopping.

We can see a handicapped person and that one can touch our hearts with compassion, yet there is nothing like experiencing these challenges on a personal level. When I see a person in a wheel chair my eyes well up with tears, my heart truly breaks, no matter the circumstance. I cannot contain my sorrow when I see one and I know that they have been like this for years or that their condition may be permanent. I think to myself, that was me and that could have been me forever.

Of all of the things I had to deal with and conquer, the helplessness that I felt in that wheel chair will be with me forever. The wheel chair affected me more than looking down at my useless legs and body. It touched me in a way I didn't expect, it hurt me. Sometimes reality will hit you right in the face in ways you and others will not expect. This was my reality every time I sat down in a wheel chair and some one else had to pilot me about.

I soon went from the motorized cart to holding onto the shopping cart. I loved it. I had to go slow, yet I was standing and was becoming independent!! How good it is!! Time quickly marched forward with more days turning into more weeks and weeks into months.

Every day I worked so very hard and soon there came a time when I could hold onto Farris and walk through the stores. Then the day came when I could walk alone, slowly, but alone and pick my own items with no assistants. I had to be very careful, because my strength was getting better, yet my balance was so unsteady. As long as I didn't turn quickly and took deliberate steps, I was fine!! It seemed that sometimes Farris was uncertain that I should be trying these new freedoms without his help. He stayed close, yet I didn't ever fall, I stumbled many times, but I learned early on how to catch myself.

It seemed in the beginning of walking unassisted, I stumbled most of the time. I concentrated on every step to maintain my balance. As long as I kept my thoughts on walking, I did pretty well, although I walked just like a drunk person. I attempted to walk forward, yet my body would weave to the side. It became second nature to learn to walk in spite of this. If a person didn't know me, I am sure it appeared that I had been drinking or high on something. I was very amused by this.

One of the mornings that I was walking up to get the newspaper, which took quite a while, because of the length of our driveway, my legs became very unsteady and began to tremble from fatigue. The mailbox is across the road and as I approached the road I saw that a car was coming, which caused me to loose my concentration on walking, I began to lean and walk just as a drunk person. The person in the car waved and I raised my hand to waive and nearly lost my balance and fell side ways and forward. I had to laugh to myself. I am sure that person thought that I was inebriated at this early hour. To this day, I get a good laugh out of that vision. Oh what a sight that must have been!!

I had several bladder infections due to having the catheter in for so long. I so badly wanted to be rid of this appendage, yet my bladder wasn't working and until it did, I would have to depend on it. I went to Urgent Care to get antibiotics to clear up the infection and to get a new catheter.

Everywhere I went, I had to carry the catheter. Farris and I found a cloth purse to put it in and it wasn't as noticeable, yet I knew that it was there. One morning I woke up not feeling good at all. Farris took me to the Emergency Room to have me checked out. They found another bladder infection. UTIs can make you feel terrible. The emergency room doctor asked if I would like to try to go with out the catheter. I was jumping with joy!! It was a very tense moment for me. There was always the question if I could ever go without the catheter. I had very few fears, yet this was one of them and probably one of the biggest fears that I had. The doctor removed the catheter and within minutes I was going on my own!!! This was the first time in about 5 months. I was shouting with pure joy!! I felt as if I were on cloud 9 when I left that hospital!! While I was in the UofL hospital they tried to wean me from the catheter, but my bladder couldn't work, so I had to continue using it. No one knew if or when my bladder would function again. I have never been so happy to pee in my life!!! It was cause for celebration!!! This is one more victory and one more question answered!!

The time came for me to see Dr. Haislip again. It was May 18th, 2010. I hadn't seen her since leaving OMHS on January 21. I was proud of how far I had come in 5 months. By this time I was walking, with a strange gait, yet I was walking and so proud of that fact. I had many questions concerning new issues I didn't understand. Since I had been getting on my feet, my feet were swelling to a point I could not wear shoes. The swelling not only involved my feet, but my legs too. I was wondering if this was going to be a permanent condition. She didn't think it would be and explained how the nerves were not working to promote muscle movement and circulation. I understood that. It was so good to see her again. We discussed what the neurologists had said about the devastation to the nerves in my legs. I relayed to her that the neurologists were doubtful that I would walk again and said if I did, it would be 2 to 3 years.

Joyce A. Haislip, M.D., P.S.C.
920 Frederica Suite 306 Owensboro, KY 42301

Date: 05/18/2010

REASON FOR VISIT: This   that I am seeing in followup for Guillain-Barre.

HISTORY OF PRESENT ILLNESS: She was admitted in January. She received IVIg and when she did not respond as well as we had hoped and the disease progressed, we shipped her off to Louisville. She received IVIg up there again I think twice.

She currently is able to walk. She is numb from the shoulder blades down. She actually can't feel. She tells me that her motor nerves, they did EMGs up there, where totally destroyed. They did not expect her to be able to walk ever again. She has been home maybe a month or so at this point and time. She could not sit up in bed when she went home. So she has worked very hard getting to where she is now. She is having swelling in her legs whenever she is up for any period of time and did not understand how that could happen. I explained to her the interaction between her nerves and her blood vessels and her muscles and why they are not responding that gravity is taking charge, and how she needs to counteract this.

Also, her left eye palpebral fissure still does not close fully. The right does at this time. An ophthalmologist that she saw in Louisville wanted to stitch her eyelid close. She declined but at that time neither one of her eyes would close. I suggested that she get back in touch with an ophthalmologist. She now lives in Indiana and have them put a gold ingot in the upper lid that will help weight the lid so that she will be able to close it with very little difficulty.

She was concerned that her fingernails were turning a little bit blue, but I reviewed that with her today and that is not the case. We fill out a form for discharging her loan application for school. I filled that out and they never received it. Apparently they lost it, so they sent a new one for me to fill in and I will take care of that for her.

PHYSICAL EXAMINATION:

VITAL SIGNS: Blood pressure: 120/70. Temperature: 97.9. Respirations: 20. Heart rate: 84.

GENERAL: Her HEART is regular rate and rhythm. Her LUNGS are clear.

ASSESSMENT AND PLAN:
1. Followup of Guillain-Barre: See discussion above. I will see her back in 4 months. She is really doing very well.

Joyce A. Haislip, M.D.
JAH/bdh

I felt so much better after seeing Dr. Haislip. She is my hero. So many people that have Guillain-Barre Syndrome are misdiagnosed and/or it takes valuable time to determine what the true condition is. With GBS every minute can determine life or death. Dr. Haislip knew with in minutes of talking with me that I have GBS.

She told me that her specialty was to become a Neurologist and she excelled in neuro medicine. I truly thank God that she was my doctor. This is the second time she rescued me from the clutches of a devastating and grave illness. Yes, she is my HERO!!

I have something to say concerning our Physicians and our relationships with them. There are all kinds of love that we as humans can feel and express. We would be dead inside if we didn't. I am not talking about anything weird or clingy. The love I speak of is one of trust, respect and appreciation. I love Dr. Haislip as my physician for all that she has done for me with genuine care and the highest standards of intellect and professionalism. She is the example of what all Physicians should be in every aspect of caring for each patient. Oh, what a different world of patient care it would be if physicians followed her example.

I personally know several of her patients and every patient that she had feel as I do. As with any and all professions, there are those who are average, and then there are those that are great... Dr. Haislip is the greatest!!

I worked hard every day to regain my ability to walk with no supports and in time I could walk a good distance, keep my balance and strength and my stamina was good. The independence of being able to use our legs is so amazing!! How often do we ever stop and think about what it would be like to lose the use of our legs. We don't think on those terms and that is good... yet I know.

Spring turned into summer and Dr. Haislip said it would be o-k for me to use the zero turn mower to mow grass. I was so happy!! I could sit on the seat of the mower and enjoy the out doors with little physical exertion. It was something I could do and not be concerned about losing my balance. I placed a box with a pillow on top on the footrest of the mower, so I could sit with my feet elevated. This helped to keep the swelling down in my feet and legs. It looked odd, but worked great!! It was rejuvenating to be able to be outside and not struggle to accomplish being there. I was in heaven feeling the air and sun in my face. What a gift!! I can do this!!!

Dr. Joyce Haislip

Dr. Haislip encouraged me to write this book. She stated that there is not a lot of information about the effects of GBS, the patient's experiences and personal needs. She explained that any information that I may share could be helpful to health care professionals and care givers providing patient care for GBS.

Dr. Haislip was one of the most personable doctors that I have ever had. Any time that I needed to see her, she always took her time to listen and address any issues that I may have. She ended every visit with this question, "Is there anything else that you would like to talk about?"

My last visit with Dr. Haislip was May 18, 2010. Little did I know that would be my last visit... all future appointments were cancelled due to her illness. Dr. Haislip passed away on February 16, 2011.

On that last visit, she and I discussed this book. She again encouraged me to write about my personal experiences with GBS. At Christmas 2010, I sent her a Christmas card and a note telling her that I would send her the first completed copy of this book.

Dr. Haislip passed after the book was finished, yet not in print. This brings a great sadness to me. The light of the medical professional's community has dimmed with her passing. Dr. Haislip's words of encouragement and kindness will be with me always. She is a true champion.

Message without Words

When I look around me what do I see... unspoken messages capturing me. The flowers, the trees, the sky... messages without words, at times no sound, messages of the Truth abound. I search the colors and He is there, I feel the breeze 'tis a whisper, an unspoken message of His grace... no words, yet I am aware. "Sunlight, oh sunlight, do guide me, 'tis messages so bright, no words need be, for His warmth is the surrendering of me." A heart need no voice to hear, to know, to feel, to see, for all around are unspoken messages... His loving presence knows all needs. His lovely whispers are all things good... for all around I can see, His messages without words ever speaking to the spirit me.

By: Shari Ka, 2005

It was time be thinking about some kind of exercise routine. I belong to the YMCA… yet I didn't think I was ready for that. I decided to start walking again. Before GBS, I walked from 1 to 3 miles a day. I knew that I shouldn't try to walk, but the minimum to start with, because walking was still a challenge.

I started with a walk that is probably a little more than ½ of a mile. I did this nearly every other day for about a week. It was very slow going and difficult, because I still don't have feeling in many areas of my feet, legs, back and chest. When I walk it feels as though I have weights on my legs and feet, as well as the areas with a sensation that I cannot describe. It almost feels swollen, yet it is not. I guess it feels as if the areas that are without feeling are raised. My legs and body is stiff, especially my legs at times do not want to bend. On this beautiful, sunny day I was ready for my walk. I knew that my legs were stiffer than normal, yet most of the time they loosened somewhat after walking awhile. On this day, they did not get better with my walk. I didn't give it a lot of thought, because, as with any thing, some days are better than others. I was on my way back home, in spite of the stiffness; I was enjoying the beauty of all of the nature in this area. We live in a partially rural area that is thick with woods, hills and all kinds of nature to enjoy. I love taking long walks. This is when I do my best thinking and spend time alone with God and all of His wonderful gifts of nature.

I came to the steep hill right before my driveway and as I started up the hill I noticed that my legs no longer wanted to move. I was getting concerned, because I have always been able to challenge myself and keep pushing and go the extra mile, but on this day, it was as if my brain and my legs had disconnected.

I was a little startled by this, especially the fact that I was on a desolate area of the county road alone and with no one near to help, should I get into trouble or maybe meet up with some one I don't want to deal with. I mentally pushed and pushed myself up that hill. I wasn't sure what I should do, but finally I made it up the hill and into my driveway. I was so relieved!! I decided then, that I was pushing my body too hard, too soon. I backed off and changed my walking schedule to about 2 times a week and that proved to be a great place to start.

The summer of 2010 was good to me. I worked hard to earn a lot of my strength back. I have not been able to do all of the things I once did; yet I am happy as to what I have achieved. I busied myself with painting birdhouses, planting flowers and playing with my dogs. During the summer I regained much of my balance. Most of the time I walk as if there are no physical limitations. Outwardly you cannot see the physical disabilities. They are there, yet if I concentrate on my steps and if I don't get into a hurry, I am fine.

I felt so good during the summer months. Every day I woke up and thanked God that He has healed my body enough that I can walk and at least be some of who I used to be. On my good days I now drive my car alone, which is a freedom of unexplainable joy! I am still having problems with my eyes. Sometimes they burn and hurt so badly that I cannot see enough to deal with traffic. I have learned to take it a day at a time. I am just happy to be able to drive as often as I do.

Night driving is impossible. I have to keep lubricants in my eyes, which causes a glare when lights shine ahead of me, it is blinding. About mid-fall I thought I was ready for an outing all alone. I wanted to see some friends in southern Indiana, so I got into my car and away I went. Everything went fine!! I had timed it so I would be home before dark. It was getting late in the fall and I didn't allow for the fact that it was getting dark earlier. Darkness came as I was heading home, yet I thought that I would be fine. While I was driving on the winding roads going through southern Indiana, I was nearly blinded every time a car came towards me due to the lights in my eyes. I panicked. I didn't think I was going to be able to make it home. I kept my eyes on the white line at the side of the road. I fallowed it and that is the only thing that saved me. I learned my lesson. Until my eyes heal, I will not drive at night again.

Summer past, then fall and now it is winter. The cold of winter has been very hard for me. The cold has brought a lot of stiffness and pain in the areas that I still have numbness. Some days it is almost like a set back. It is very difficult to walk and I awake each morning in pain. I look forward to warmer weather.

In a couple of weeks it will be the anniversary of my diagnosis. January 12, 2010 I was diagnosed with Guillain-Barre Syndrome and little did I know that my life would change forever. Little did I know that I was in for a fight for my life. As I sit here I am truly amazed as to what can occur in a years time. Events unimaginable!! I look back on it and even I am impressed with what I lived and fought my way through.

I am far from whole again, yet I am miles from where the symptoms started and January 12th 2010 the date of my diagnosis. I still have difficulty walking, although most times it is not apparent to those around me. My legs and feet are only about ½ awake.

I have very little feeling in the middle of my back all the way down my legs. My rib cage area is only partially awake. There is some feeling there, yet not at a normal level. The right side of my face is close to normal, but the left side is still partially paralyzed. My left eye closes only part of the way, unless I make it close. My speech is impaired at times due to the nerve damage in my face, especially my mouth and tong.

The doctors say that what ever you regain after 2 years is the best you will be. I am at one year now, so I have realistically one more year to try to regain the rest of my body. The fight is still on. I will never stop trying. I want to get my smile back. I have a funny crooked face and I really am o-k with that, but I want to be able to smile again and not have the focal point of my face be ½ of my mouth not moving. At this date, this is my goal. I think it will come back, maybe not all of the way, but at least enough that I can smile with out all eyes looking at the paralyzed side of my face.

Does it upset me that people look to my mouth every time I smile? No, it doesn't, because I understand. No one does this to be mean; it is just a natural response. I may have done the same thing. I don't recall if I have, but I am sure that I have with no thought of hurting any one.

When my tong and face get lazy, as it does sometimes, I guess it is difficult for others to understand me. I am unaware of this until I notice that I am asked several times," what did you say," which happens a lot. I have worked hard to exercise my face, yet it seems to be recovering

46

slowly from the paralysis. I am not discouraged by this. I just keep working on it with hopes I will regain the left side of my face in the near future. There are no guarantees for recovery with GBS.

One of the things that bother me and are kind of silly. I have days when my legs are stiff and I have a difficult time walking. On those days I park in the handicap parking area. When I get out of my car, it appears that I am walking o-k, yet I have to move deliberately and slowly. I can't tell you how many times I have been given the eye, because I don't appear to be handicapped. If I have learned anything it is this, don't judge a book by it's cover!! On the days that I feel strong enough, I don't use the handicap parking area, which is a lot of the time.

On the days that I am having problems, I do use the handicapped parking area. If you see a person in the handicap parking area and they appear to be healthy, that doesn't necessarily mean that they are… if one is walking slowly over the crosswalk, be patient, for they may be walking as fast as their ability allows them to walk… if one isn't speaking clearly, gently ask if they will repeat what they have said… most importantly, never look at the disabled area of one's body, look the person in the eyes and smile …never turn away.

It has been a tough year and a tougher journey, yet I am here and writing this book. I have a long way to go, but from here in comparison to where I was a year ago, the remainder of my journey should be a piece of cake.

We never know when we get out of bed in the morning what the day has in store for us. One day I was making candy and reading books, seemingly healthy and with-in hours I lost it all. Every increment of my independence was gone. I feel that I have been given a second chance at life, which I literally have been. There are many folks with GBS that have not recovered or their recovery wasn't as successful as mine has been… I am blessed and every day I know this with every cell in my body, I am so very blessed. God heard all of the prayers for me and He answered them in the most wonderful way, and against all odds, I am walking again!!

I am hoping that my body will completely heal and I will continually work towards that goal. If I don't get better from here, then I will be o-k with what I have now, because I am so very blessed, I am completely independent and I am walking again!!

My face has recovered, with the exception of a slight weakness that remains on the left lower area of my face. It is somewhat apparent when I smile, but when I am not smiling it is not noticeable. Outwardly my physical disabilities do not show. I have a long way to go; yet I would rather think of it, as I have come a long way since January 2010.

If I Were a Butterfly …

What would I feel…
I would fly all around
with such grace and zeal.

I would find each flower,
I'd choose each one,
not caring the color,
'tis nectar, taste'n fun.

If I were a butterfly
what would I feel…
the damp morning dew,
the afternoon sun.

I'd dance through the air
'til darkness come.
I'd hide in folded wings
when day is done.

If I were a butterfly
what would I feel...
as I dip and soar,
I'd fly so high
'til I was no more!!

By: Shari Ka, 2000

My recommendations for providing patient care for GBS.

I had several health care workers and my doctor, ask me to comment on what procedures I thought may be helpful for the care of those with GBS.

GBS is an uncommon illness, therefore many health care workers and home care providers either have never cared for a patient with GBS or may care for a GBS patient for the first time. Due to damage to the sensory nerves, a GBS patient will experience pain and sometimes severe pain, which will require handling unique to burn patients.

The most important addition that I can add to the care that I received was that all healthcare workers and/or home care providers should physically handle the patient, as if they are a burn patient. Due to the sensory nerve damage, the GBS patient has the sensation of being burned over most or all of the body. It is important that those handling the body of a GBS patient, do not apply pressure by using a closed hand grasp. Lift the limbs with an open hand, allowing the limb to rest on the open palm as often as possible. This method spares the patient a great deal of pain.

I highly recommend memory foam mattresses or like material for the GBS patient to lay on. Any other mattress surfaces add to the patient's discomfort. Any mattress with a textured surface or solid surface should not be used. Air mattresses with ribbed surfaces should not be used due to the uneven hard surface. Even the slightest crease in the sheets can cause a great deal of pain, therefore the ridges of the air mattress only adds to the discomfort of the patient. The air mattresses are used to allow air circulation to help prevent bedsores. It would be better to be turned more often for the prevention of bedsores than to lay on a mattress that adds to the discomfort of GBS nerve damage.

As I have mentioned in the book, I had a nurse at UofL, that had worked several years in the burn unit. It amazed me, as to her ability to handle my body causing the least amount of pain.

As with any person with illnesses and/or injuries to this magnitude, health care workers and/or home care providers should understand the psychological trauma the patient most likely is dealing with. A great deal of empathy is needed during the patient's transition from a healthy person to a disabled person. There is not any one thing that can be done or said to change the patient's situation, yet compassion and understanding is a must, for this person has lost their previous life. With this loss the patient may feel the devastation of emotions and the uncertainties that this loss creates. A professional, which deals with the psychology of these traumas, would have been helpful for me early on. I suggest that a trained Social Worker or trained counselor to counsel the patient, so the patient can have an outlet for any and all obvious concerns due to the trauma of such a destructive illness. Helplessness oft times manifests confusion, frustration and sometimes fear. Confusion is usually a manifestation of unanswered questions. This should be dealt with as early as possible. The physical body may have changed, but psychologically one is still the same person inside